AMICUS ILLUSTRATED • AMICUS INK

DO YOU REALLY WANT TO MEET A WEASEL?

WRITTEN BY CARI MEISTER   ILLUSTRATED BY DANIELE FABBRI

Amicus Illustrated and Amicus Ink
are published by Amicus
P.O. Box 1329
Mankato, MN 56002
www.amicuspublishing.us

Copyright © 2019 Amicus. International copyright reserved in all countries. No part of this book may be reproduced in any form without written permission from the publisher.

Library of Congress Cataloging-in-Publication Data
Names: Meister, Cari, author. | Fabbri, Daniele, illustrator.
Title: Do you really want to meet a weasel? / by Cari Meister ; illustrated by Daniele Fabbri.
Description: Mankato, Minnesota : Amicus, [2019] | Series: Do you really want to meet ... ? | Audience: K to grade 3. | Includes bibliographical references.
Identifiers: LCCN 2017039253 (print) | LCCN 2017053181 (ebook) | ISBN 9781681514758 (pdf) | ISBN 9781681513935 (library binding) | ISBN 9781681523132 (pbk.)
Subjects: LCSH: Weasels–Juvenile literature.
Classification: LCC QL737.C25 (ebook) | LCC QL737.C25 M3775 2019 (print) | DDC 599.76/62-dc23
LC record available at https://lccn.loc.gov/2017039253

Editor: Rebecca Glaser
Designer: Kathleen Petelinsek

Printed in the United States of America

HC 10 9 8 7 6 5 4 3 2 1
PB 10 9 8 7 6 5 4 3 2 1

ABOUT THE AUTHOR

Cari Meister has written more than 200 books for children, including the TINY series (Viking), and the FAIRY HILL series (Scholastic). She lives in Edwards, Colorado, with her husband, four sons, a goldendoodle named Koki, and an Arabian horse named Sir William. Find out more at carimeister.com.

ABOUT THE ILLUSTRATOR

Daniele Fabbri was born in Ravenna, Italy, in 1978. He graduated from Istituto Europeo di Design in Milan, Italy, and started his career as a cartoon animator, storyboarder, and background designer for animated series. He has worked as a freelance illustrator since 2003, collaborating with advertising agencies and international publishers, and has illustrated many books for Amicus.

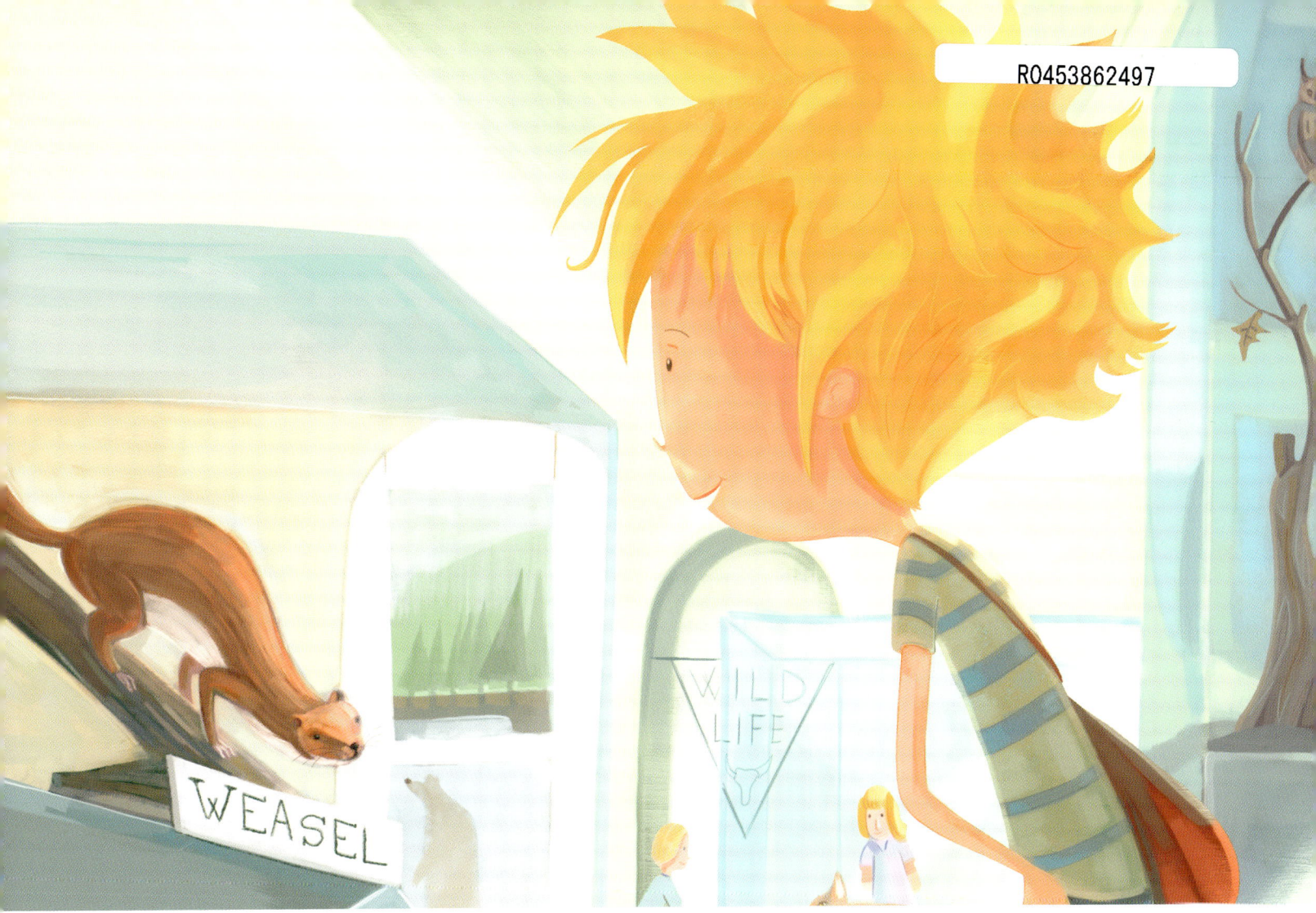

Weasels are small, furry, and cute. But did you know they are the world's smallest meat-eating mammal? These sweet-looking creatures can kill prey larger than themselves!

What's that? You want to meet a weasel in the wild? Are you sure? Did you know that a weasel kills the same way a jaguar does? It bites the back of its victim's neck. This pierces the animal's skull or spinal cord.

Did you *also* know that the weasel has a very stinky weapon? It's true. If a weasel is cornered, it will release yellow gunk from under its tail.

Scientists call it musk. It stinks! It scares away predators, such as coyotes. You still want to meet a weasel?

Okay. Weasels are not hard to find. They live all over the world. Different species live in different places. The least weasel and the short-tailed weasel live in North America, Europe, and Asia. The long-tailed weasel lives in North and South America.

You can usually find an animal if you know what it eats. The long-tailed weasel eats gophers, moles, voles, and field mice. They live in areas with soft dirt good for tunneling—places like fields and grasslands.

Do you see any clues? There are some clumps of earth.
Oh! It's a gopher hole. Look around. Are there any weasel tracks around the hole?

A weasel has small, hairy paws with five toes. The inside fifth toe does not always show up in the track. And the tracks are only about ½ inch (1.25 cm) long. Are those weasel tracks? Yes! Follow them!

The tracks stop at this hole. What is that to the side of the hole? It looks like a pile of. . . scat!

Congratulations! You found a weasel home. This weasel lives in an old underground mole burrow. Weasels also make dens under tree roots or in rotting logs.

Now find a place not too far from the den, but not too close. Sit and watch. The weasel will come out to hunt soon. Weasels have to eat often because they can't store fat. Ah! There he is. But what is he doing? He is bopping back and forth in front of a gopher.

It is a "war dance" meant to confuse the gopher. The weasel runs, jumps, and even somersaults! The gopher freezes. He is not sure what to do.

Then, the weasel strikes! He bites the back of the gopher's neck. The gopher dies instantly.

The weasel eats its brain. Then he carries the carcass back to his den. He will store the leftovers to eat later. Now you have really met a weasel!

WHERE DO WEASELS LIVE?

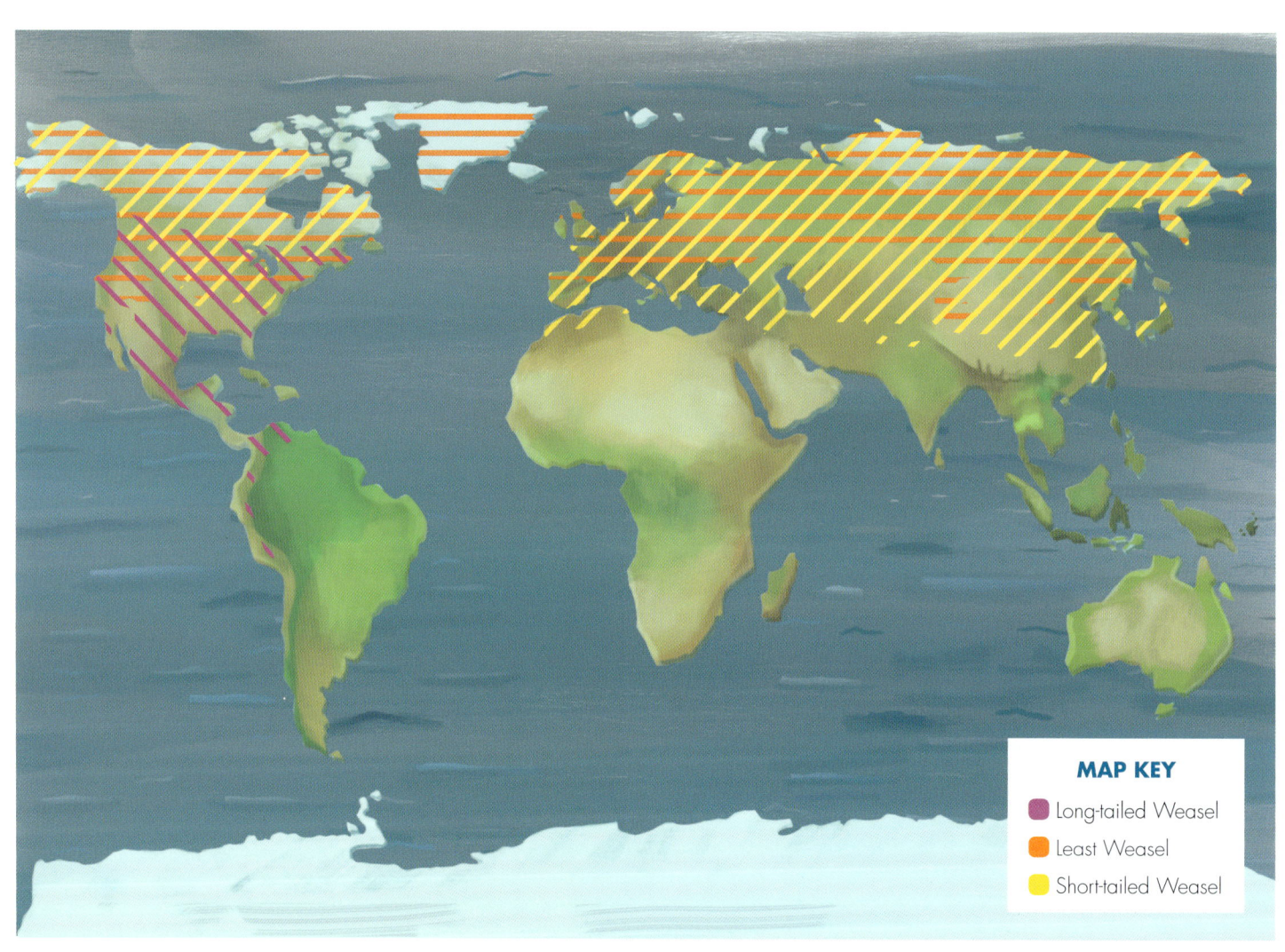

22

GLOSSARY

carcass The body of a dead animal.

mammal An animal that has fur and gives birth to live young.

predator An animal that hunts another animal for food.

prey An animal that is hunted by other animals.

scat Poop of a wild animal, often used in tracking.

spinal cord A group of nerves that run through the spine.

vole A small rodent related to the mouse.

READ MORE

Borgert-Spaniol, Megan. Weasels. Backyard Wildlife. Minneapolis: Bellwether Media, 2012.

Levine, Michelle. **Mammals.** Animal Kingdom. Mankato, Minn.: Amicus, 2015.

Royston, Angela. Mammals. Chicago: Heinemann Raintree, 2015.

WEBSITES

Bio Kids Critter Catalog: Long-tailed Weasel
http://www.biokids.umich.edu/critters/Mustela_frenata/
Read up on fun facts about the Long-tailed weasel.

DK Find out! : Weasels
https://www.dkfindout.com/us/animals-and-nature/weasels/weasels/
Learn all about weasels and their relatives, including minks, stoats, martens, and more!

The Least Weasel: National Geographic
http://www.nationalgeographic.org/media/least-weasel/
Watch a video of a least weasel hunting.

Every effort has been made to ensure that these websites are appropriate for children. However, because of the nature of the Internet, it is impossible to guarantee that these sites will remain active indefinitely or that their contents will not be altered.